Marley to the Rescue

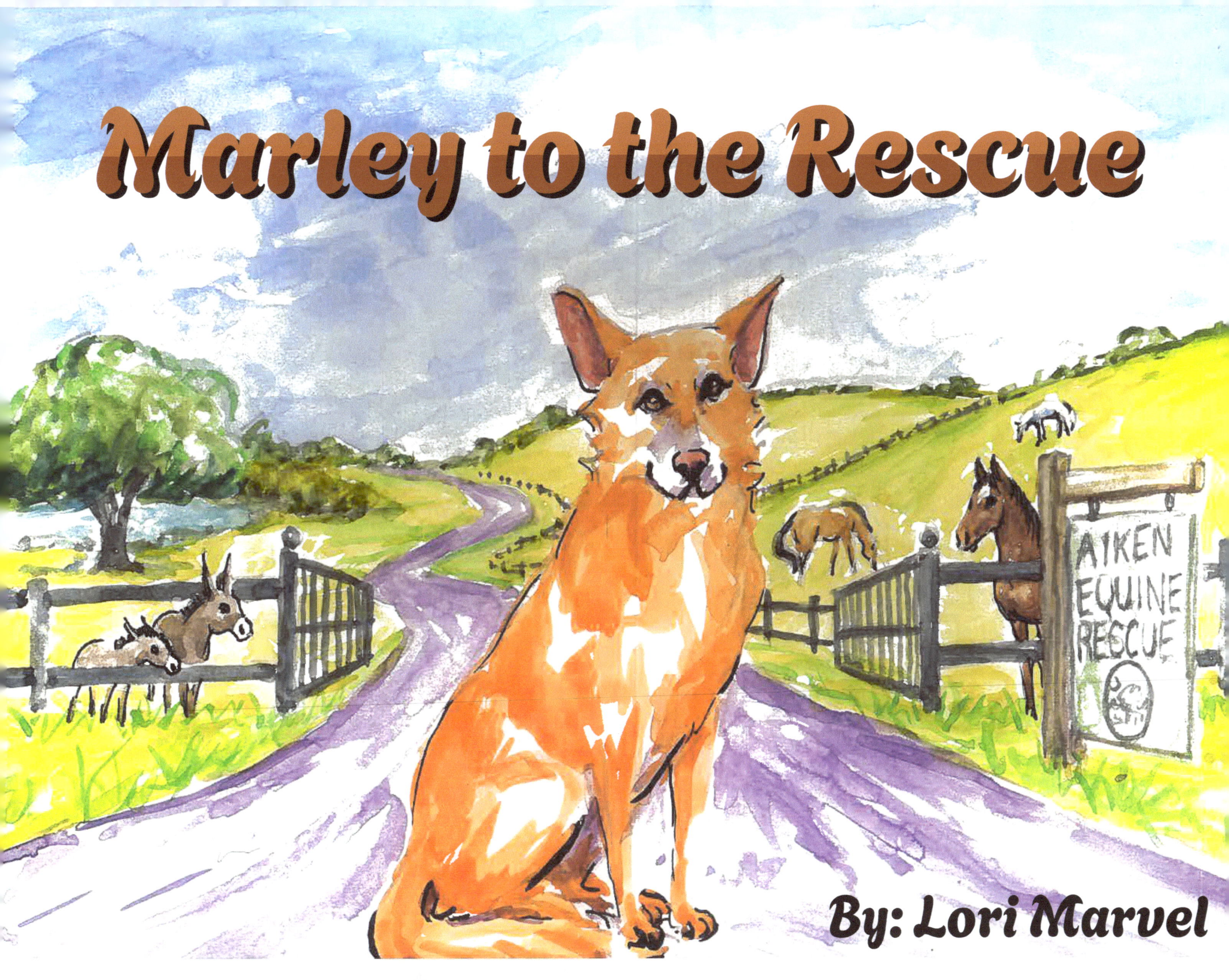

By: Lori Marvel

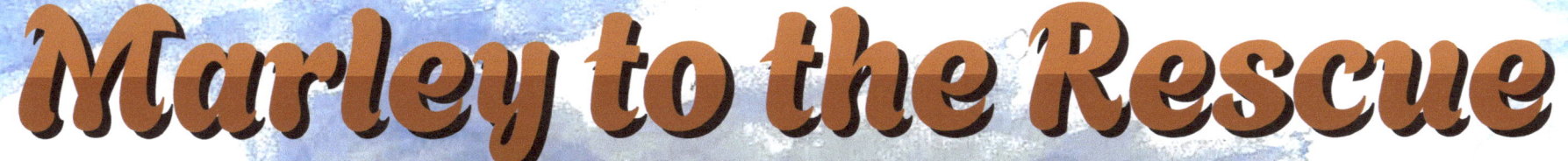

Dedication

In loving memory of all the horses, who have touched our hearts deeply, and to all the devoted volunteers who love and selflessly care for God's creatures at the Aiken Equine Rescue.

Your dedication and compassion continue to inspire and heal.

Acknowledgements

My deepest gratitude goes to Ellen Valentino, our talented illustrator. Ellen's remarkable artistry, equestrian skills, and dedicated volunteer work at the Aiken Equine Rescue have brought this book to life.

A heartfelt thank you to Ken Yates, our diligent editor. Ken has published numerous children's books in his retirement, finds joy in volunteering at the Aiken Equine Rescue, and his editorial expertise has been invaluable.

About the Author

Lori Marvel, is a dedicated volunteer at the Aiken Equine Rescue, an Aiken resident, a talented interior designer, and a local realtor. Her passion for helping animals and her deep connection to the Aiken community shine through in her writing.

**This is a story about a very special dog named Marley.
Marley is a hard-working farm dog.**

She takes care of horses, ponies, donkeys, cats and anyone who just needs a friend.

Marley starts her day greeting and checking on all the new horses, ponies, and donkeys that come to her farm. The morning air smells like sweet hay, and the sun shines on the green pastures.

Marley dashes across the field, her paws kicking up little clouds of dust as she hurries to greet the newcomers.

She talks to them and tells them this is a safe new home and not to be afraid.

"Hey there, friend" Marley barks cheerfully, her tail wagging with excitement. "Welcome to the Aiken Equine Rescue! Tell me, what's your story? What happened to you? Where did you come from?"

"My name is Chester," the new horse says. "I used to pull a very heavy cart. One day, my owner said he didn't need me anymore."

"Oh, don't worry, friend!" Marley exclaims, her eyes shining with warmth. "You are in the best place in the world!"

"You'll love it! I'll get Jane, and she'll make you feel much better.

In the morning,
Ashley will fill your bucket
with a delicious breakfast.
Okay, gotta run. New arrivals coming!"

"Hi friend. My name is Marley," she barks warmly. "Welcome to the best place in the whole world! Where are you from?"

"My name is Greased Lightning," the horse replies with a proud flick of his mane. "I used to run really fast. One day, I hurt my leg. Then my owner decided it was time for me to retire."

"Oh, that's okay," Marley says. "We have lots of horses just like you. I'll introduce you to some new friends. You're going to love it here." Marley cheerfully yelps, " See you soon."

"This is our duck, Homer. Homer is a special duck, and he'll show you where the best grass is!"

Marley whispers softly to the scared horse, "Remember, you're safe here. You're loved, and you're never alone."

Marley spends all day greeting the new horses, her tail wagging furiously as she makes sure each one feels loved and welcomed. She nuzzles their noses and whispers kind words, making their first day a cheerful day.

When she finally grows tired, Marley trots over to find her best friend, Shiloh, the farm cat. Together, they curl up under her favorite tree, a grand old oak whose branches stretch out like caring arms. The soft rustling of leaves and the gentle sway of the branches create a soothing lullaby. As Marley nestles against Shiloh's soft fur, she sighs happily.

Marley listens to the soft breezes and the horses neighing in the pastures. She whispers to Shiloh, "This is the best place in the world."

One of Marley's favorite things to do on the farm is to help the volunteers with tours.

Kris, a favorite volunteer of Marley's, laughs and says, "Marley let the guests sit on the seats."

When Marley jumps off to the floor and rests her head on her feet, Kris says, "Good job, Marley; now let's show these nice people where all our horses live. We'll visit Taco and Margarita first to give them their carrots."

Some days Marley's job is really hard.

She tirelessly runs around the farm, always ready to lend a comforting paw or a friendly nuzzle. Whether it's a horse feeling lonely, a pony needing reassurance, a donkey seeking a friend, or a volunteer needing a hug Marley is there. Her kind eyes and gentle presence offer a sense of security and warmth to everyone she meets.

Marley softly whispers into a sick horse's ear, "It will be okay friend; I'm here. Remember what I told you. This is the best place in the world."

One day, Marley awakened to a noise louder than she has ever heard. She heard her human

Momma's frantic voice yelling, "FIRE! FIRE! Save the pony."

Marley's heart raced as she watched her Momma run down the hill and rush into the burning barn.

She was so scared.

Fear gripped Marley's chest.

Out came her Momma and a pony named Whistle, who was covered in soot and so scared he could hardly move.

Marley and her Momma watched as the fire trucks raced up the hill.
She had never seen anything like this before.
Marley shivered as her Momma held her close.

That evening, Marley walked with her Momma and Dad. They checked every horse, donkey, bird and cat on the farm and told them, "We'll be okay."

Marley whispered softly to each one, "Don't worry, Remember what I told you. You are in the best place in the world. You are safe, and you are loved. Just wait and see what's next."

Then Marley overheard her Dad saying, " We're going to build a new barn, even bigger and better than anything we ever had. We'll help even more horses find new homes, and it will be the best place in the world!"

Prologue

Horses, ponies and donkeys continue to come to the Aiken Equine Rescue and get the care they need. Veterinarians provide medicine, farriers provide new shoes, and with the help of the TAA (Thoroughbred Aftercare Alliance), our horses are rehomed and given new careers.

Events like our Pony Pals kids' summer camps provide learning, education and fundraising for the new barn.

Thoroughbred Aftercare Alliance. We have earned the Thoroughbred Aftercare Alliance "Marquis" status for rehabbing, retraining and rehoming off-the-track Thoroughbreds. We place in the top 1% nationally for equine rescues.

Guidestar Charity - 2024 Platinum Status - Candid

"Marley to the Rescue" tells the heartwarming story of Marley, a real-life farm dog who embodies the spirit of a cherished thoroughbred horse rescue in Aiken, South Carolina. Marley brings the thoughts and feelings of the horses and animals to life, sharing their stories with readers. With her endearing farm dog instincts, Marley gently guides and cares for the horses. Together with her friends and a special cat named Shiloh, Marley helps these retired and responsibly surrendered horses and donkeys find new purpose and joy in their lives.

www.ingramcontent.com/pod-product-compliance
Lightning Source LLC
Chambersburg PA
CBHW050848010526
44107CB00017BA/1215